Year 1 English — CGP's got it covered!

Practice makes perfect in Year 1 English, so we've assembled this book to make sure pupils have all the practice they need. All the key topics are here — SPaG, Comprehension and Writing — fully matched to the National Curriculum.

If that wasn't enough, we've also included progress tests throughout to easily keep track of how they're doing. And with answers at the back, it's simple to check if they really know their stuff.

What CGP is all about

Our sole aim here at CGP is to produce the highest quality books — carefully written, immaculately presented and dangerously close to being funny.

Then we work our socks off to get them out to you — at the cheapest possible prices.

Contents

About This Book 1

Start of Year One Test 2

Section One — Grammar

Forming Sentences 6
Joining Words with 'and' 8
Joining Sentences with 'and' 9
Mixed Grammar Practice 10

Section Two — Punctuation

Capital Letters for Names and 'I' 11
Capital Letters and Full Stops 12
Separating Words with Spaces 13
Question Marks and Exclamation Marks 14
Mixed Punctuation Practice 16

Section Three — Spelling

The Alphabet 18
Consonant Pairs 19
Vowel Sounds 20
The 'ch', 'sh' and 'th' Sounds 24
Words with 'ph' and 'wh' 25
The Hard 'c' Sound 26
Words Ending in 'ff', 'll', 'ss' and 'zz' 27
Words Ending in 've' and 'nk' 28
Words Ending in 'tch' and 'ch' 29
Adding 's' and 'es' to Words 30
Adding 'ing', 'ed', 'er' and 'est' to Words 31
Adding 'un' to the Start of Words 32
Syllables and Compound Words 33
Tricky Words 34
Mixed Spelling Practice 36

Progress Test 1 39

Section Four — Reading

Finding Information 42
Thinking About Words 44
Making Assumptions 46
Putting Things in Order 48
What Happens Next? 50
Mixed Practice — Stories 52
Mixed Practice — Information Texts 55
Mixed Practice — Poems 58

Progress Test 2 60

Section Five — Writing

Writing Lower-Case Letters 64
Writing Capital Letters and Numbers 68
Writing Stories 70
Describing Things 72
Writing About Real Life 74

End of Year One Test 76

Answers 80

Published by CGP

Editors:
Aimee Ashurst, Keith Blackhall, Emma Crighton, Nathan Mair, Hannah Roscoe

ISBN: 978 1 83774 052 9

With thanks to Emma Duffee, Nathan Mair and Lucy Towle for the proofreading.
With thanks to Jade Sim for the copyright research.

Images on the cover and throughout the book © Educlips
Clipart from Corel®

Printed by Elanders Ltd, Newcastle upon Tyne.
Based on the classic CGP style created by Richard Parsons.

Text, design, layout and original illustrations © Coordination Group Publications Ltd. (CGP) 2023
All rights reserved.

Photocopying this book is not permitted, even if you have a CLA licence.
Extra copies are available from CGP with next day delivery • 0800 1712 712 • www.cgpbooks.co.uk

About This Book

This Book is Full of Year 1 English Questions

This book has questions for the topics in Year 1 English. It covers grammar, punctuation, spelling, reading and writing.

Some pages have Warm Up Questions to get you started on the topic.

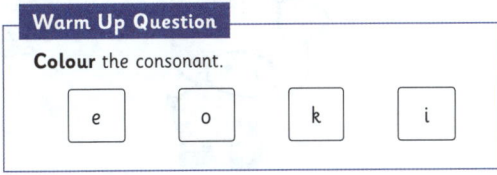

Some pages have Now try this activities at the end. These will give you an extra challenge.

There are Four Tests in This Book

There is a Start of Year One Test at the front of the book, so you can see what you already know about English.

There are two Progress Tests. Each one tests you on all the topics that have come before it. They help you see how you're doing with the topics covered so far.

There is an End of Year One Test at the back of the book. This helps you to practise what you've learnt in Year 1.

Use the Smiley Faces to Show How Confident You Feel

There are smiley faces at the end of each topic.

Tick here if you're really struggling.

Tick here if you need a bit more practice.

Tick here if you can do all the questions on the page.

Start of Year One Test

1 **Circle two** things that contain the 'ee' sound.

 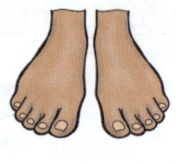  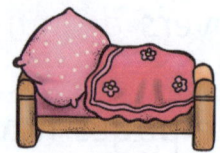

2 marks

2 **Draw lines** to **match** each picture to the correct spelling.

   quack

quick

1 mark

3 **Read** each word. Then circle the **correct** picture.

swing

train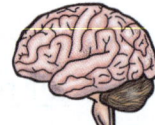

2 marks

Start of Year One Test

④ Circle the **two** things Olivia needs.

"I need a hat and a scarf."

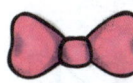 

2 marks

⑤ Circle the **capital letter** and **underline** the **full stop** in each sentence.

Scarlett loves toast.   Yusuf is out today.

2 marks

⑥ Rearrange the letters in the boxes to make words. Use the **pictures** to help you. The first letter of each word is in **bold**.

   **p** l a t n

....

   **s** l p s h a

....

2 marks

Start of Year One Test

7 **Look** at the pictures.
Tick the sentence that matches each picture.

Jack is looking at that map. ☐

Jack has lost his map. ☐

We are at the airport. ☐

We are at the funfair. ☐

2 marks

8 **Draw lines** to match each sentence to the correct picture.

a)

b)

c)

That is her little kitten.

She is singing a song today.

The king has a crown.

2 marks

Start of Year One Test

9 **Read** the story below. Put the images in **order** to match the story, using the numbers 1 to 3.

> Sam set off in his rocket. He went through space and then landed on the Moon.

☐   ☐   ☐

_____
3 marks

10 **Write two** words to **describe** each picture on the lines.

The cupcake is ....

and ....

The girl is ....

and ....

_____
4 marks

Score: ☐ /22

Section One — Grammar

Forming Sentences

Warm Up Question

Tick the sentence that makes sense.

I play with my cat. ☐

With play cat my I. ☐

1 **Read** each sentence. **Circle** 'yes' or 'no' to show whether the sentence **makes sense**.

Henry very sleeps well.   Yes   No

Kate makes lots of food.   Yes   No

2 **Join** the parts of the sentences so they **make sense**. The first one has been done for you.

This cake —————————— do tricks.

I wash ———————————— tastes great.

Dogs can ————————————— my hands.

Forming Sentences

3 **Fill** in the gaps so that these sentences **make sense**.

Rashid a sails boat.

Rashid .... boat.

Lucy the ball throws.

Lucy .... ball.

4 **Rearrange** the words in the **boxes** to form **sentences**.

| took | plane | The | off |

....

| is | very | kind | She |

....

Joining Words with 'and'

1 **Cross out** the '**and**' that is **not** needed in each sentence.

Her hair and is short and curly.

The dragon has and a tail and wings.

I play and rugby and football.

Tim loves and hamsters and gerbils.

2 **Tick** the box where '**and**' should go in each sentence. The first one has been done for you.

My skirt ☐ is pink ✓ purple.

Henry ☐ Meera are ☐ doctors.

The sky ☐ is grey ☐ cloudy.

Lola ☐ plays the trumpet ☐ the piano.

Joining Sentences with 'and'

① **Join** the parts of the sentences so they **make sense**. The first one has been done for you.

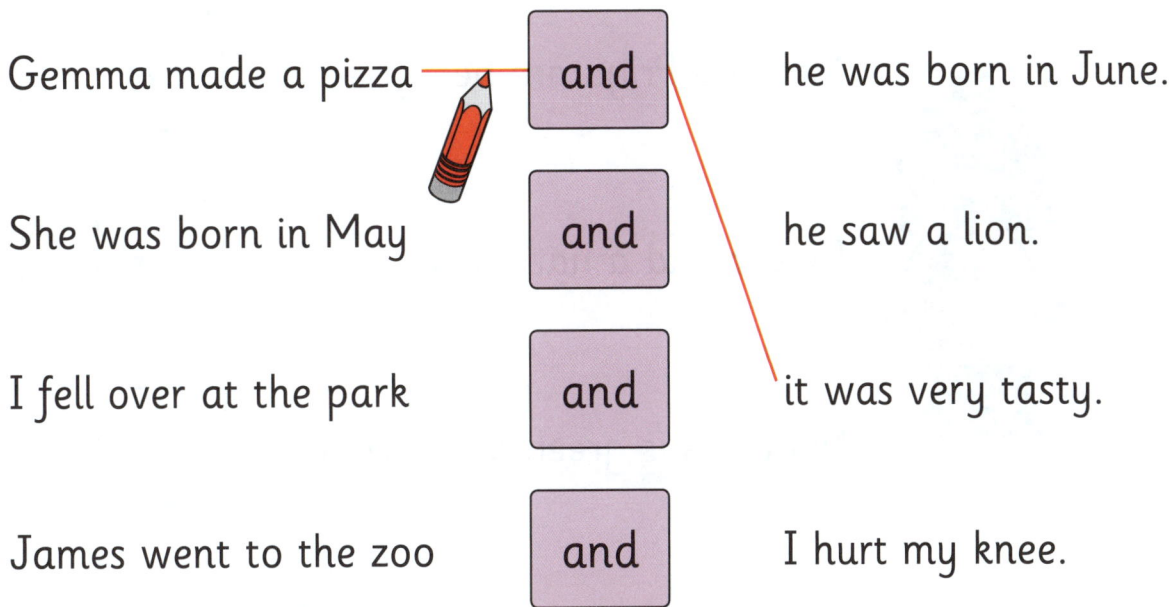

Gemma made a pizza — and — he was born in June.

She was born in May — and — he saw a lion.

I fell over at the park — and — it was very tasty.

James went to the zoo — and — I hurt my knee.

② **Join** each pair of sentences together using '**and**'. **Write out** the new sentences on the lines.

Samira likes apples. Josh likes pears.

....

....

The teacher is speaking. They are listening.

....

....

Mixed Grammar Practice

1 **Circle** 'yes' or 'no' to show whether each sentence uses '**and**' correctly.

Mia and Priya are best friends.   Yes   No

I wear and a hat gloves.   Yes   No

My dress is green and stripy.   Yes   No

2 **Rewrite** this sentence so that it **makes sense**.

Liam large a snowman makes.

....

....

3 **Rewrite** this sentence, adding '**and**' in the correct place.

I kicked the ball it flew over the fence.

....

....

Section Two — Punctuation

Capital Letters for Names and 'I'

1) Read each pair of sentences. **Tick** the sentence that uses **capital letters** correctly.

Freya loves Bert. ☐

freya loves Bert. ☐

It is monday. ☐

It is Monday. ☐

I live in london. ☐

I live in London. ☐

Tom and I are tall. ☐

Tom and i are tall. ☐

2) Read each sentence. **Underline** the word that should have a **capital letter**.

Sanjana went to wales with Ben.

Julia had a party on saturday.

Peter and i live in Oxford.

3) Rewrite the sentence below, adding **capital letters** in the correct places.

sam and omar read books.

....

Capital Letters and Full Stops

1 **Colour** 'yes' or 'no' to show whether each sentence uses **capital letters** and **full stops** correctly.

Mum works in a museum.   Yes   No

my house is on a big hill.   Yes   No

Jenny. is an amazing person.   Yes   No

2 **Tick** the **two** sentences that use **capital letters** and **full stops** correctly.

My arm is sore. ☐   Tamara has a nap ☐

it is a lovely day. ☐   Matt wants a biscuit. ☐

3 **Rewrite** the sentence below using a **capital letter** and a **full stop**.

the tractor has huge wheels

....

Now try this

Write a sentence about where you live.
Remember to use capital letters and full stops correctly.

Section Two — Punctuation

Separating Words with Spaces

1 **Read** each pair of sentences. **Tick** the sentence that uses **spaces** correctly.

Myshoes aremuddy. ☐   It is a tasty pie. ☐

My shoes are muddy. ☐   It isa tastypie. ☐

2 **Rewrite** the sentences below using **spaces**. Use the **pictures** to help you.

Jakewinsagoldmedal.

....

....

Iridemybiketoschool.

....

....

Millyhidesbehindawall.

....

....

Question Marks and Exclamation Marks

Warm Up Question

Colour the question mark **red**.

Colour the exclamation mark **blue**.

① **Write** either a **question mark** or a **full stop** in the box to finish each sentence.

Where are you ☐   The clown is funny ☐

Wes is one year old ☐   Who is that man ☐

Lea's hat is blue ☐   How is the weather ☐

② **Read** each pair of sentences. **Tick** the sentences that could end with an **exclamation mark**.

I am so happy ☐   Can we play outside ☐

Are you happy too ☐   It is such a nice day ☐

What a strange hat ☐   How fun this is ☐

Why is it so long ☐   Is that fun ☐

Section Two — Punctuation

Question Marks and Exclamation Marks

3) **Colour** '!' or '?' to show whether each sentence should end with an **exclamation mark** or a **question mark**.

What a good climber Rob is [!] [?]

How high is that wall [!] [?]

How very brave Rob is [!] [?]

When can I try rock climbing [!] [?]

4) **Rewrite** each sentence, adding either an **exclamation mark** or a **question mark** on the end.

Do you like my wellies

....

How far away are you

....

What a large chicken this is

....

Section Two — Punctuation

Mixed Punctuation Practice

1 **Circle** 'yes' or 'no' to show whether each sentence uses **spaces** correctly.

Shewalks for miles.   Yes   No

Rahman boils the kettle.   Yes   No

Whata good idea!   Yes   No

I had a great day.   Yes   No

2 **Circle** the words that **always** need a **capital letter**.

paris   fishing   aisha   scotland

town   luke   home   february

Rewrite the words you circled, giving each one a **capital letter**.

Section Two — Punctuation

Mixed Punctuation Practice

 3 **Read** each sentence. **Underline** the word that should start with a **capital letter**. Then add a **full stop** to the sentence.

Julie runs a restaurant in <u>manchester</u>.

The first one has been done for you.

 Her brother frank is the chef

They are always busy on friday evenings

Mum and i love the pizzas at the restaurant

 4 **Rewrite** each sentence, making sure you put a **capital letter** in the correct place. **Add** either an **exclamation mark** or a **question mark** to finish each sentence.

when does the train leave

....

how bright that star is

....

Why is alexis so cross

....

Section Three — Spelling

The Alphabet

Warm Up Question

Colour the consonant.

| e | o | k | i |

1 **Draw** lines to show whether each letter is a **vowel** or a **consonant**. The first one has been done for you.

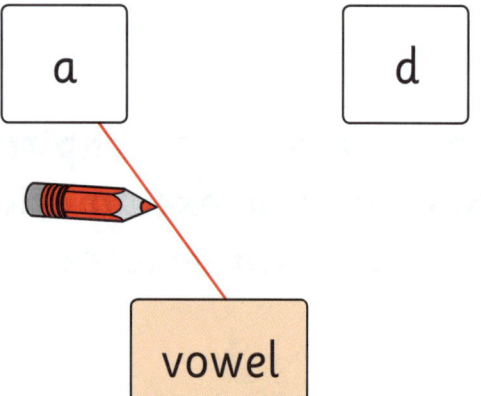

| a | | d | | u | | g |

vowel   consonant

2 **Write** the missing **vowel** in each word below so that it matches the picture.

tr.........p   h.........g   l.........mp

Consonant Pairs

1 **Circle** the letters that are **missing** from each word. The first one has been done for you.

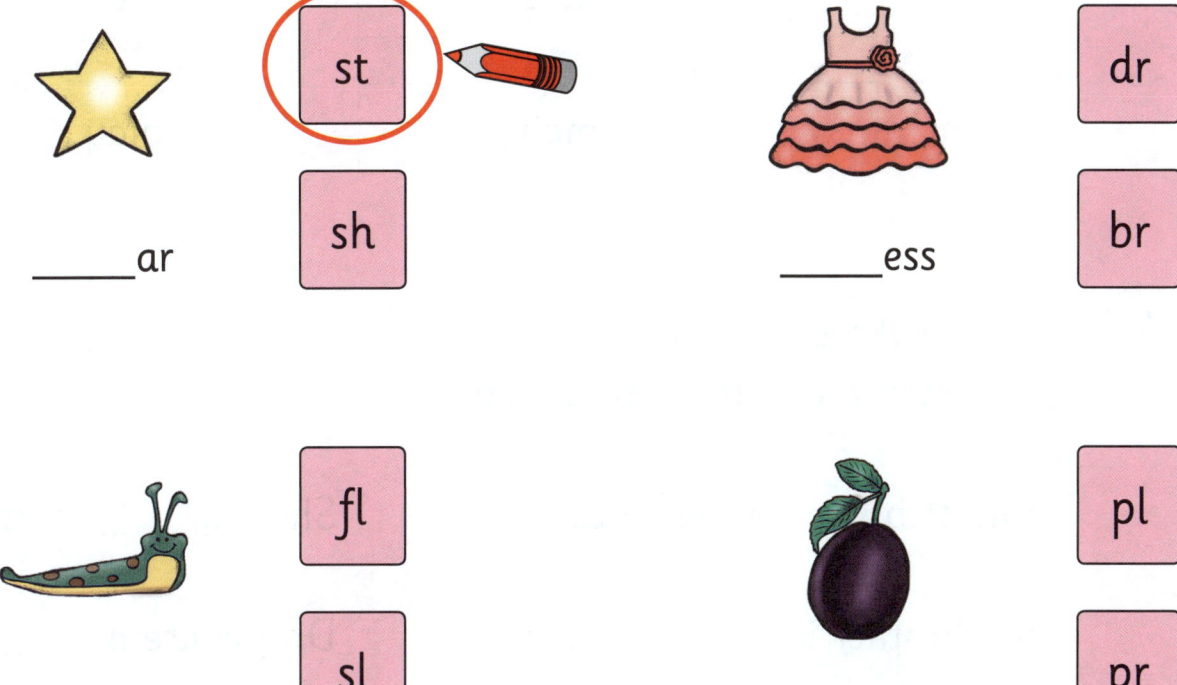

2 Choose a **consonant** from the box to complete each word below. You can only use each letter **once**.

Section Three — Spelling

Vowel Sounds

1) Tick the word in each pair that is spelt **correctly**.

crane ☐   mayl ☐   plai ☐

crayn ☐   mail ☐   play ☐

2) Fill in the gap in each sentence with either '**oi**' or '**oy**'.

I must b..........l the kettle.

She enj..........s running.

My brother is ann..........ing.

Drums are n..........sy.

3) Draw lines to match the words to the **correct** missing letters. The first one has been done for you.

str____m — ea

sh____ld

lad____

ie

bab____

dr____m

y

th____f

Section Three — Spelling

Vowel Sounds

4 **Circle** the correct spelling of the word in **bold**.

My rucksack is quite **light** / **lite**.

Taj **tried** / **tride** to climb the fence.

5 **Cross out** the words that are **spelt incorrectly**.

food   flewe   gloo

true   blew   chue

6 **Rearrange** the letters in the boxes to complete the words. Use the **pictures** to help you. The first one has been done for you.

Christopher will **g**row............ a plant. | w o r |

We are travelling on a **b**................. . | a t o |

The dog can't find his **b**................. . | e o n |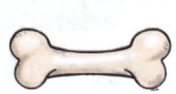

Section Three — Spelling

Vowel Sounds

7 **Cross out** the word in each pair that is spelt **incorrectly**.

wul / wool   mune / moon   rules / rools

8 **Circle** the letters that are missing from the words below.

h____d   ea   e   fr____n   ow   ou

p____ncil ea   e   l____d   ow   ou

9 **Complete** the words with the correct missing letters.

ur   ir   er

I saw a **flow**............... in the garden.

My sister has **c**...............**ly** hair.

Timmy is covered in **d**...............**t**.

Now try this

Can you write down three more words that end in 'er'?

Vowel Sounds

10 **Draw** lines to match each picture to the **correct spelling**.

alarm
alarrm

drore
draw

sore
sor

lornch
launch

11 **Colour** 'yes' or 'no' to show whether the words in bold are spelt **correctly**.

Can you **heer** the music?   Yes   No

We are working in **pares**.   Yes   No

The **bear** has brown fur.   Yes   No

The shop is **near** the cinema.   Yes   No

Section Three — Spelling

The 'ch', 'sh' and 'th' Sounds

> **Warm Up Question**
>
> **Circle** the correct letters to complete the word below.
>
> ____ark   ch   sh

1 **Draw** lines to match the words to the **correct** missing letters.

 fi____   th

 lun____   sh

 ____umb   ch

2 **Look** at the pictures. **Fill in** the gaps with either '**ch**', '**sh**' or '**th**'.

............eese   ....eep   ba............

Section Three — Spelling

Words with 'ph' and 'wh'

1 **Colour** the letters that are missing from the words below.

dol___in | ph | | f | ___eekend | wh | | w |

2 **Circle** the **correct spelling** of the word in **bold** in each sentence below.

I can say the **alphabet / alfabet** backwards.

The **whater / water** is very cold today.

Use the **wisk / whisk** to mix the eggs.

3 **Complete** the name of each object starting with '**ph**' or '**wh**' by writing the missing letters on the lines.

wh..................

ph..................

ph..................

wh..................

Section Three — Spelling

The Hard 'c' Sound

1 **Cross out** the word in each pair which is spelt **incorrectly**.

sik / sick   korn / corn   sock / sok

2 **Rearrange** the letters in the boxes to complete the words. Use the **pictures** to help you. The first one has been done for you.

m ask   k s a

s ....   l c a e

t ....   a r k c

3 Each of these words is spelt **incorrectly**. **Write** the **correct** spellings on the lines.

karrot ....   citten ....

aktor ....   luky ....

Words Ending in 'ff', 'll', 'ss' and 'zz'

1) **Tick three** words that are spelt **correctly**.

leaf ☐   fluf ☐

seall ☐   hill ☐

bel ☐   sniff ☐

2) **Write** '**ss**' or '**zz**' to complete each word.

fi...............   che...............   gra...............

Now try this

Can you think of any more words that end with 'ff', 'll', 'ss' or 'zz'? Write them down on a piece of paper.

Section Three — Spelling

Words Ending in 've' and 'nk'

1 **Underline** the words that are spelt **correctly**.

arryve   abuve   tank

drink   behave

2 **Circle** the **correct** spelling of the word in **bold** in each sentence below.

The witch lived in a dark **kave / cave** .

Harmony cleaned the **sink / synk** .

I bit a **chunk / chunnk** out of the apple.

Larry has **twelvve / twelve** pairs of sunglasses.

3 **Draw** lines between the letters in each box to spell a word ending in 've'. The first letter of each word is in **bold**. The first one has been done for you.

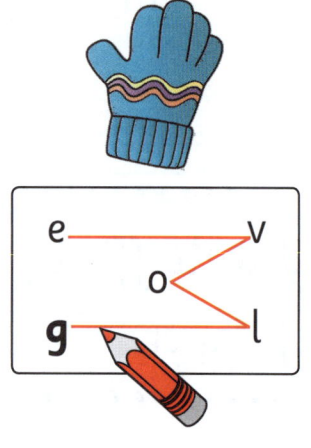

e v		e d		h o
o		r		s
g l		v i		e v

Section Three — Spelling

Words Ending in 'tch' and 'ch'

1) **Read** each sentence. **Colour** the letters missing from the word in **bold**.

He uses a **cru**.... to help him walk.   tch   ch

Karina couldn't **rea**.... the top shelf.   tch   ch

Galia waited for the chicks to **ha**....   tch   ch

2) **Complete** the words in the sentences below. Use the **pictures** to help you.

The monkey swings on the bran....................

I play fe........................ with my dog at the park.

Julia is relaxing on the bea.......................

Section Three — Spelling

Adding 's' and 'es' to Words

1 **Cross out** the word in each pair that is spelt **incorrectly**.

peachs   peaches      coates   coats

2 **Draw** lines to match each word to the correct **ending**.

path   splash

s

dragon   tent

es

fox   cross

3 Rafa has written a shopping list.
Rewrite the list so there's **more than one** of each item. The first one has been done for you.

flower
box
apple
dress

.... *flowers* ....

....

....

....

Section Three — Spelling

Adding 'ing', 'ed', 'er' and 'est' to Words

1   **Circle** the correct word to complete each sentence.

Tina is [braver] [bravest] than Victor.

The birds are [singer] [singing] in the trees.

Hattie has the [neatest] [neated] handwriting.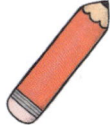

We [waiter] [waited] outside the cinema.

2   **Add** the **endings** to the **words**. **Write** the new words on the lines.

small + est   cook + ing

....

want + ed   quick + er

....

Section Three — Spelling

Adding 'un' to the Start of Words

1 **Colour** the word where '**un**' has been added **correctly**.

unndo   untie   unzzip

2 **Add** '**un**' to the words below so that they mean the **opposite**.

...........fit   ....tidy   ....fold

3 Add '**un**' to each of the words below.
Write the new words on the lines so that each sentence **makes sense**. Use each word **once**.

happy   fair   safe

The creaky ladder looked very ....

The .... pig walked home slowly.

"That is so ....!" shouted Frances.

Section Three — Spelling

Syllables and Compound Words

1 **Draw** lines to match the words to the correct number of **syllables**. The first one has been done for you.

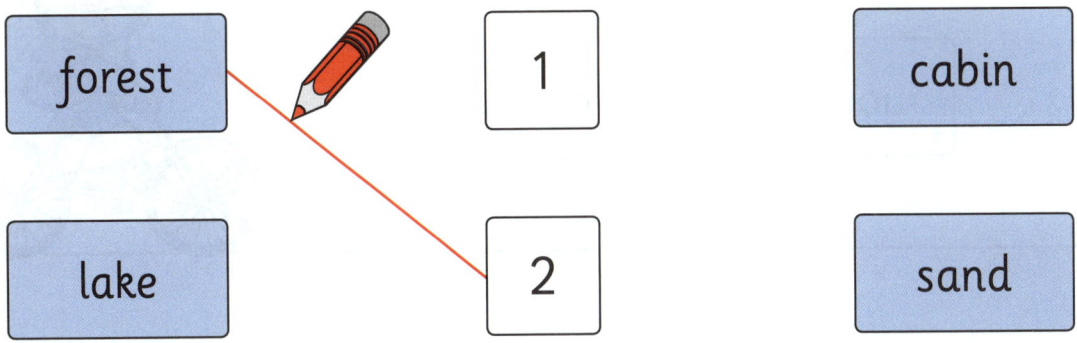

2 **Write** how many **syllables** each word has in the box.

coconut ☐   wood ☐   walrus ☐

banana ☐   unicorn ☐   doctor ☐

3 **Look** at the words below. They can be **joined together** to make **new words**. **Write** the new words on the lines.

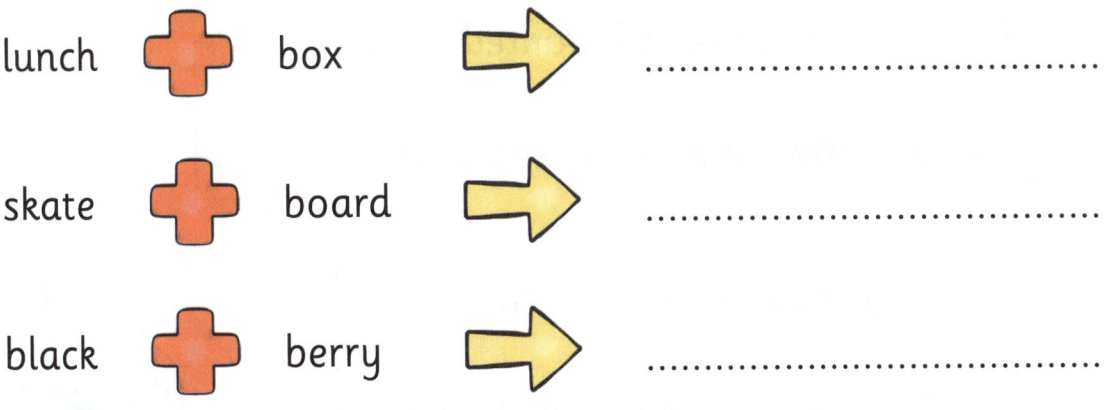

Section Three — Spelling

Tricky Words

Warm Up Question

Colour the word that is spelt **correctly**.

| your | yor |

1 The blue words are spelt **incorrectly**. **Colour** the option that shows the **correct** spelling of each word.

onse   once   onece

luve   love   luv

2 **Read** each pair of sentences. **Tick** the one where the word in **bold** is spelt **correctly**.

Malaya asked **what** I wanted to eat. ☐

Malaya asked **wat** I wanted to eat. ☐

The **litul** mouse hid from the cat. ☐

The **little** mouse hid from the cat. ☐

Tricky Words

3 **Read** the sentence below. **Underline** the word that is **not** spelt correctly.

My best frend lives on a farm.

4 In each of these sentences, the word in **bold** has been spelt **incorrectly**. **Write** the **correct** spellings on the lines.

Please help me **moove** the chair. ....

Dilip invited me to his **howse**. ....

That is a **pritty** picture on the wall. ....

5 **Circle** the **correct** spelling of each word in the box. **Write** the word in the correct sentence.

where / wair   sed / said   skool / school

Jakub walks to .... in the morning.

I could not remember .... it was.

The teacher .... it was lunchtime.

Mixed Spelling Practice

1 **Circle** the word that is spelt **correctly** in each pair of words.

higher   kindist   faster

highher   kindest   fastter

2 **Complete** the words in **bold** by **colouring** in the correct missing letters.

The shop sells cakes, pies and **br** | ea | ee | **d**.

I enjoyed the **stor** | ie | y | about robots.

Anwar was very **m** | ee | ea | **n** to his brother.

3 **Draw** lines to match the words to the correct missing letters.

in___   mar___   pa___   swi___

tch   ch

Section Three — Spelling

Mixed Spelling Practice

4 Circle the letters that are missing from each word.

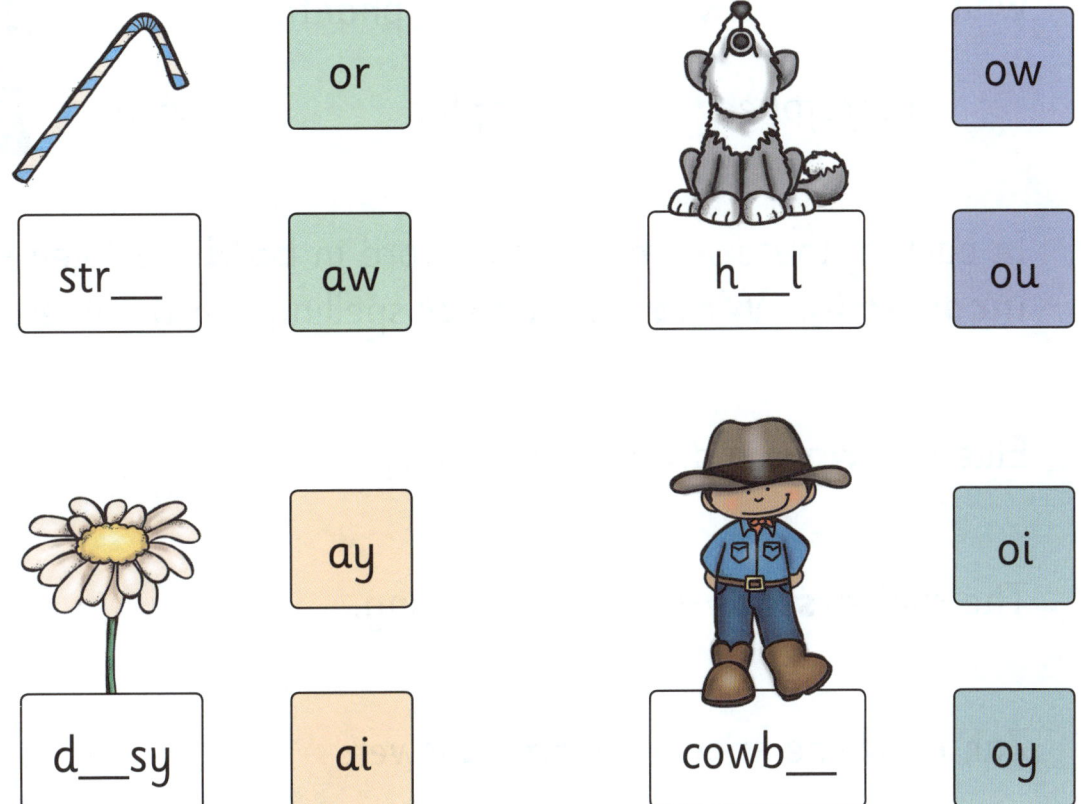

5 Rewrite these words so that there is **more than one** of each item The first one has been done for you.

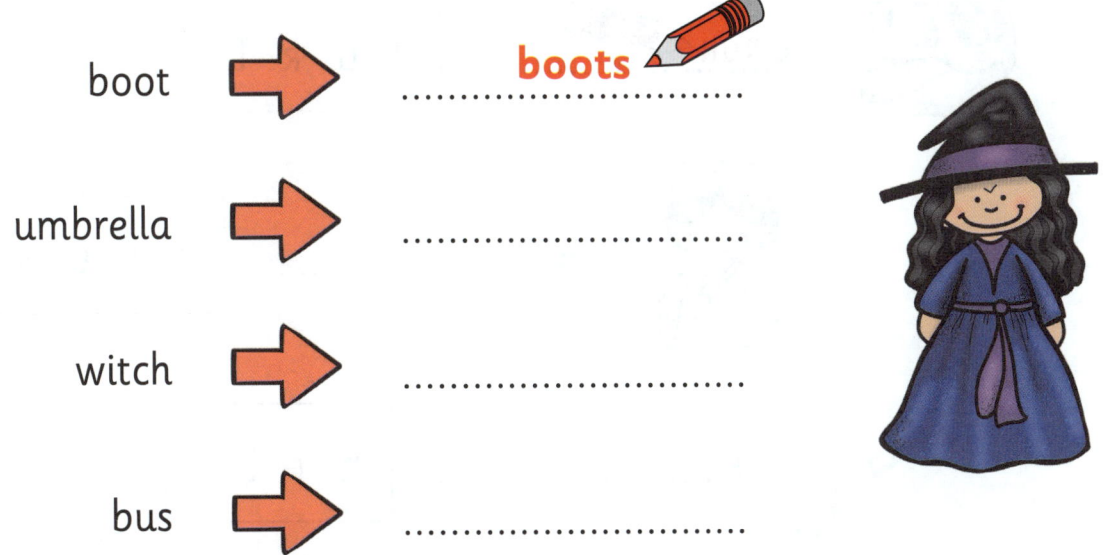

boot → **boots**

umbrella → ....

witch → ....

bus → ....

Mixed Spelling Practice

6 **Cross out** the words that are spelt **incorrectly**.

white   whedding   phantastic

microfone   trophy   whip

7 In each of these sentences, the word in **bold** has been spelt **incorrectly**. Write the **correct** spellings on the lines.

Ellie will **ware** a dress to the party. ....

The robber **stoal** a famous painting. ....

Zak thinks he knows the **rite** answer. ....

8 **Rearrange** the letters in the boxes to complete the words. Use the **pictures** to help you. The first one has been done for you.

s kull | l u k l |

n.................. | e r u s |

s.................. | k t i c |

Section Three — Spelling

Progress Test 1

1 **Tick two** sentences that use '**and**' correctly.

Sophia likes and singing dancing. ☐

My brother is intelligent and kind. ☐

The bee has black and yellow stripes. ☐

Jamal has and two cats and a fish. ☐

2 marks

2 **Draw** lines to match each word to its missing letters.

___ild

___rone

fre___

ch

sh

th

2 marks

3 **Circle** the words that are spelt **correctly**.

treat   skigh   cownt   scene

shert   care   awai   bite

4 marks

Progress Test 1

Progress Test 1

4 **Cross out** the words that are **spelt incorrectly**.

playing   wished   walkked

jumpped   yawning   stayying

3 marks

5 **Read** these sentences. **Write** the **correct** spellings of the words in **bold** on the lines.

I found a **shel** on the beach. ....

Joe's hamster is **kute**. ....

Fatima is **fiv** years old. ....

3 marks

6 **Tick** the word in each pair that is spelt **correctly**.

dishs ☐   dishes ☐

plants ☐   plantes ☐

catch ☐   cach ☐

3 marks

Progress Test 1

Progress Test 1

7 **Circle** the correct spelling to complete each sentence.

The weather is terrible **tooday / today** .

Li **unwraps / unnwraps** his presents.

Would you like **sum / some** vegetables?

3 marks

8 **Colour** 'yes' or 'no' to show whether each sentence uses **punctuation** correctly.

What a funny film that was!	Yes	No
What size are your new boots!	Yes	No
What do you want for lunch?	Yes	No

3 marks

9 **Rewrite** the sentence below, adding **capital letters** and a **full stop** in the correct places.

amy had a party on friday

....

3 marks

Score: ☐ /26

Section Four — Reading

Finding Information

Read the story, then answer the questions.

> **Raj's Day Out**
> Raj went for a day out to the beach with his friends. They all had lots of fun. Raj used a bucket and spade to build a massive sandcastle. Grace ate a tasty ice cream. Cole lay on the sand and read a book. In the afternoon, they paddled in the sea.

1) Where did Raj and his friends go? **Tick one** box.

the park ☐   the beach ☐   the cinema ☐

2) **Draw** lines to **match** each child to the activity they did.

Raj   Grace   Cole

🍦   📖   🏰

3) What did Raj and his friends do in the afternoon?

....

Section Four — Reading

Finding Information

Read the text, then answer the questions.

Facts about Kangaroos

- Kangaroos come from Australia.
- A group of kangaroos is called a mob.
- Kangaroos use their strong back legs to leap big distances.
- Mother kangaroos have pouches on their fronts for carrying their babies.

1 **Circle** the correct option in each sentence below.

Kangaroos live in **Asia / Australia** .

A **mob / pack** is a group of kangaroos.

2 What helps kangaroos to leap big distances? **Tick one** box.

They have short fur. ☐   They have pouches. ☐   They have strong legs. ☐

3 How do mother kangaroos carry their babies?

....

Thinking About Words

Read the story, then answer the questions.

The Treehouse
Nadiya gazed up at her new treehouse. Her dad had been building it for weeks. Now it was finally finished. She speedily climbed up the ladder and went inside the treehouse. She shouted for her brother to join her, but he was too frightened to go up the ladder.

1) **Read** the first sentence. What does the word '**gazed**' mean? **Circle one** answer.

smiled   looked   danced

2) Which of these words means the same as '**speedily**' in the text? **Tick one** box.

quickly ☐   quietly ☐   slowly ☐

3) **Find** and **copy** a word from the text which means '**scared**'.

....

Thinking About Words

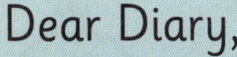

Read the diary entry, then answer the questions.

> Dear Diary,
> Today I went on a walk in the forest with my dog, Archie. We saw giant trees and lots of flowers. Archie trotted cheerfully along the path but he barked noisily when he saw a rabbit. When we got home, Archie fell asleep on my lap. We had a wonderful day!

1) What does the word '**giant**' mean in the text? **Tick one** box.

small ☐   old ☐   big ☐

2) Colour the word that means the same as '**cheerfully**'.

sadly   happily   angrily

3) Find and **copy** a word from the text which means '**loudly**'.

....

4) Find and **copy** a word from the text meaning '**very good**'.

....

Section Four — Reading

Making Assumptions

Warm Up Question

Look at the picture. **Circle** the **correct** word to **complete** the sentence.

Sophie **likes** / **hates** animals.

1 **Decide** which statement is most likely to be **true** based on the sentences below. **Tick one** box for each sentence.

Josh put on a hat and scarf before going outside.

The weather is warm outside. ☐

The weather is cold outside. ☐

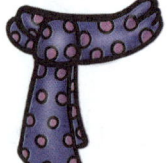 

Benjamin told a joke and Meena laughed.

Meena thought Benjamin's joke was funny. ☐

Benjamin is not very good at telling jokes. ☐

Elizabeth smiled when she saw the spider.

Elizabeth is afraid of spiders. ☐

Elizabeth likes spiders. ☐

Making Assumptions

2) **Look** at the pictures below. **Tick** the statement in each pair that is most likely to be **true**.

Chloe is going to a dance lesson.

Chloe is going to a piano lesson.

Hassan is about to start a race.

Hassan has just finished a race.

Esther enjoys the autumn.

Esther enjoys the summer.

3) **Look** at the picture and the writing. What colour T-shirt is **Aaron** wearing? **Circle one** answer.

Logan shouted as loud as he could but Aaron wouldn't listen.

yellow

red

Section Four — Reading

Putting Things in Order

1 Look at the **pictures**. Put the words in the right **order** using the numbers 1 to 3.

☐ serve	☐ peel
1 bake	☐ eat
☐ decorate	☐ grow

2 **Read** the text. Put the animals in **order** of when they appear in the story, using the numbers 1 to 3.

> First, the farmer showed us the pigs. Then, we fed the chickens. Next, we helped the farmer to herd the sheep. After that, we combed a horse's mane.

sheep ☐
pigs ☐
horse ☐

3 **Read** the text. Put the foods in **order** of when they appear in the story, using the numbers 1 to 4.

> I had some soup to begin with, then I ate a bowl of pasta. After that, I had a small salad and finally I finished the meal with some cherries.

pasta ☐   soup ☐   cherries ☐   salad ☐

Section Four — Reading

Putting Things in Order

4 Put this story in the right **order** by **drawing** lines to the correct numbers.

They found treasure buried in the sand.

1

They arrived and began to explore.

2

The pirates set sail for the island.

3

5 **Look** at the pictures and **read** the sentences. Use the numbers 1 to 3 to put the sentences in the right **order**. **Write** a sentence on the line to **describe** the final picture.

Thomas ate a big sandwich for his lunch.

Thomas walked to the park to meet his friends.

Thomas played with his basketball.

4

....

Section Four — Reading

What Happens Next?

Read the texts below and answer the questions.

> Owen got home from school and wanted a snack. He walked into the kitchen and saw a plate filled with chocolate chip cookies on the table.

1 What do you think Owen does next? **Tick one** box.

He goes to his bedroom. ☐

He eats a cookie. ☐

He goes to school. ☐

> Maisam decided that she wanted to do something nice for her mum. She walked outside and saw that her mum's car was covered in mud. Then she remembered that there was a bucket and sponge in the garage.

2 What do you think Maisam does next? **Colour one** box.

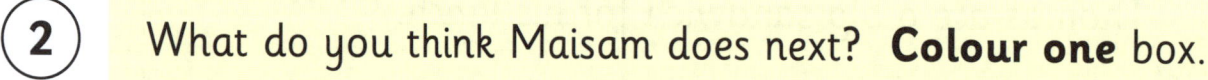

| She washes the car. | She takes a bath. | She bakes her mum a cake. |

What Happens Next?

Read the texts below and answer the questions.

> Alice and Camilo sat watching the egg. They had been waiting for weeks for the chick to hatch. Suddenly, the egg began to shake. Then a crack appeared in the shell.

3 What do you think happens next?

....

> Zara and Paul needed to cross the river. There was no bridge and it was too dangerous to swim across. Paul looked nervously at the river, wishing he had stayed at home.
>
> Zara wondered whether they should make a raft, but then she saw a boat on the riverbank which could fit one person.

4 What do you think Zara does next?

....

5 What do you think Paul does next?

....

Mixed Practice — Stories

Read the story, then answer the questions.

Ava and the Robot

After two years, Ava had finished building the robot. It was the first one she had ever made, so she felt a bit nervous.

Ava pressed a button on the back of its head and its eyes lit up. It was working! Now it was time for a test — she wanted to see if it could cook her favourite meal.

(1) How long did Ava spend building her robot? **Circle one** box.

| a year | two years | twenty years |

(2) Why does Ava feel nervous?

....

....

(3) What does Ava want the robot to do for her?

....

Mixed Practice — Stories

Read the story, then answer the questions.

Little Red Riding Hood

Little Red Riding Hood was walking through the forest to visit her grandmother. She had spent all morning making a basket full of cakes, bread and fruit to give to her grandmother.

She was strolling along the path past the trees when she met a wolf.

1) Why is Little Red Riding Hood walking through the forest?

....

2) Tick two things that Little Red Riding Hood has in her basket.

fruit ☐   bread ☐   cheese ☐

3) What does the word '**strolling**' mean? **Colour one** box.

walking   running   crawling

Now try this

Based on the text, do you think Little Red Riding Hood is a kind person? Which part of the text tells you this?

Mixed Practice — Stories

Read the story, then answer the questions.

The Alien

Jess yawned and walked upstairs. She was ready to go to sleep. She brushed her teeth, put on her pyjamas and got into bed.

Just as she started to fall asleep, she heard a strange rustling under her bed. She bent down to look underneath. She was shocked to see a tiny green alien staring back at her.

1 How does Jess feel at the **beginning** of the story? **Colour one** word.

scared   angry   tired

2 **Tick two** things that Jess does before going to bed.

puts on her pyjamas ☐   brushes her teeth ☐

reads a book ☐   looks under the bed ☐

3 **Find** and **copy** a word from the text that means '**very small**'.

....

Mixed Practice — Information Texts

Read the text, then answer the questions.

How to Grow a Plant:

1. Fill a plant pot with soil and then dig a small hole.

2. Place the seeds into the hole and cover them with plenty of soil.

3. Place the pot in sunshine and water the soil often.

4. Look out for a green shoot coming out of the soil. This means that the plant is growing.

① **Circle two** things that you **need** to follow these instructions.

② **Tick two** things that the text says plants need to grow.

water ☐   sunshine ☐   snow ☐

③ According to the text, what do you see when the plant is growing?

....

....

Mixed Practice — Information Texts

Read the text, then answer the questions.

Octopuses

- Octopuses are found in every ocean on Earth.
- They have eight long arms.
- Octopuses eat clams, crabs and small fish.
- They can change colour to hide from other sea creatures.

1 **Circle** the correct option in each sentence.

Octopuses live in **some / all** oceans.

Octopuses have eight **short / long** arms.

2 **Name two** things that octopuses eat.

....

3 Why do octopuses change colour?

....

....

Section Four — Reading

Mixed Practice — Information Texts

Read the text, then answer the questions.

Who were the Vikings?

- The Vikings came from Scandinavia, an area in the north of Europe.
- They travelled on wooden boats called longships.
- The Vikings sailed to much of Europe and America.
- Because they spent so much time at sea, the Vikings ate a lot of fish.

1 **Underline** the correct word to complete each sentence.

The Vikings were from **America / Scandinavia** .

Viking longships were made from **wood / stone** .

2 Based on the text, which of these statements do you think is **true**? **Tick one** answer.

The Vikings were bad at sailing. ☐

The Vikings were good at sailing. ☐

3 Why did the Vikings eat a lot of fish?

....

....

Mixed Practice — Poems

Read the poem, then answer the questions.

The Little Brown Mouse
The little brown mouse
Was exploring the house,
Hunting for something to eat.

He sneaked through a door,
Found baked beans on the floor,
And squeaked at the lovely treat.

1 **Tick two** words that describe the mouse.

brown ☐   white ☐   little ☐

2 What does the word '**Hunting**' mean in the text? **Circle one** word.

searching   jumping   sitting

3 What do you think the mouse does next? Give a **reason** for your answer.

....

....

Section Four — Reading

Mixed Practice — Poems

Read the poem, then answer the questions.

> ## Spring
> The chilly winter is over and done.
> Now it's spring, there is blue sky and sun.
> The flowers bloom and all the birds sing,
> What a wonderful time of year is spring!

1 **Find** and **copy** a word which means '**cold**'.

....

2 Put these things in **order** of when they appear in the poem, using the numbers 1 to 3.

3 Do you think the narrator enjoys spring? Give a **reason** for your answer.

....

....

Now try this

Write down three things you like about your favourite season.

Progress Test 2

1 **Read** the sentences. **Colour** the letters that are missing from the words in **bold**.

Would you like a **pi____a** ? | zz | ss |

He accepted her kind **o____er**. | f | ff |

The bee is **bu____ing** loudly. | ss | zz |

3 marks

2 **Rewrite** the sentence below using **spaces**.

Iclimbupthetree.

....

1 mark

3 **Circle** the correct spelling of the word in **bold** to complete each sentence.

My aunt got me a **doll / dol** as a present.

He **kicked / kikked** the ball as hard as he could.

The dress was red with **wite / white** stripes.

3 marks

Progress Test 2

4 Add '**er**' or '**est**' to complete the words in **bold** so that the sentences make sense.

He is the **fast**............ runner I know.

I am much **tall**........... than I was last year.

Fatima is the **old**........... in her class.

3 marks

5 **Rearrange** the letters in each box to make a word. **Write** the new words on the lines. The first letter of each word is in **bold**.

k **t** h n i ....

n u r **t** k ....

2 marks

6 **Rewrite** the sentence in the right order so that it **makes sense**.

want zoo You visit the to.

....

1 mark

Progress Test 2

Read the poem and answer the questions.

> **The Tree**
> Down in the woods there is a tree,
> Around ten times the height of me.
> It stands over us as we giggle and play,
> How I wish to be that enormous one day!

7 Circle the correct option to complete each sentence below.

The tree is in **a garden** / **the woods** .

The writer wants to be **taller** / **shorter** .

2 marks

8 **Find** and **copy** a word from the text which means '**laugh**'.

....

1 mark

9 What does the word '**enormous**' mean? Circle **one** option.

| very small | very big | very kind |

1 mark

Progress Test 2

Read the text and answer the questions.

> Reggie the seagull walked along the beach, watching all the children having fun. He saw a girl catching a volleyball and a boy playing frisbee with his friends.
>
> A flock of seagulls landed nearby and smiled at Reggie. One of them had a stolen frisbee in its beak. Reggie squawked with excitement.

10 **Tick two** activities that Reggie sees on the beach.

frisbee ☐   surfing ☐   volleyball ☐

2 marks

11 Do you think the flock of seagulls are friendly? Give **one** reason for your answer.

....

....

1 mark

12 What do you think happens next?

....

1 mark

Score: ☐ /21

Section Five — Writing

Writing Lower-Case Letters

Practise writing these letters neatly.

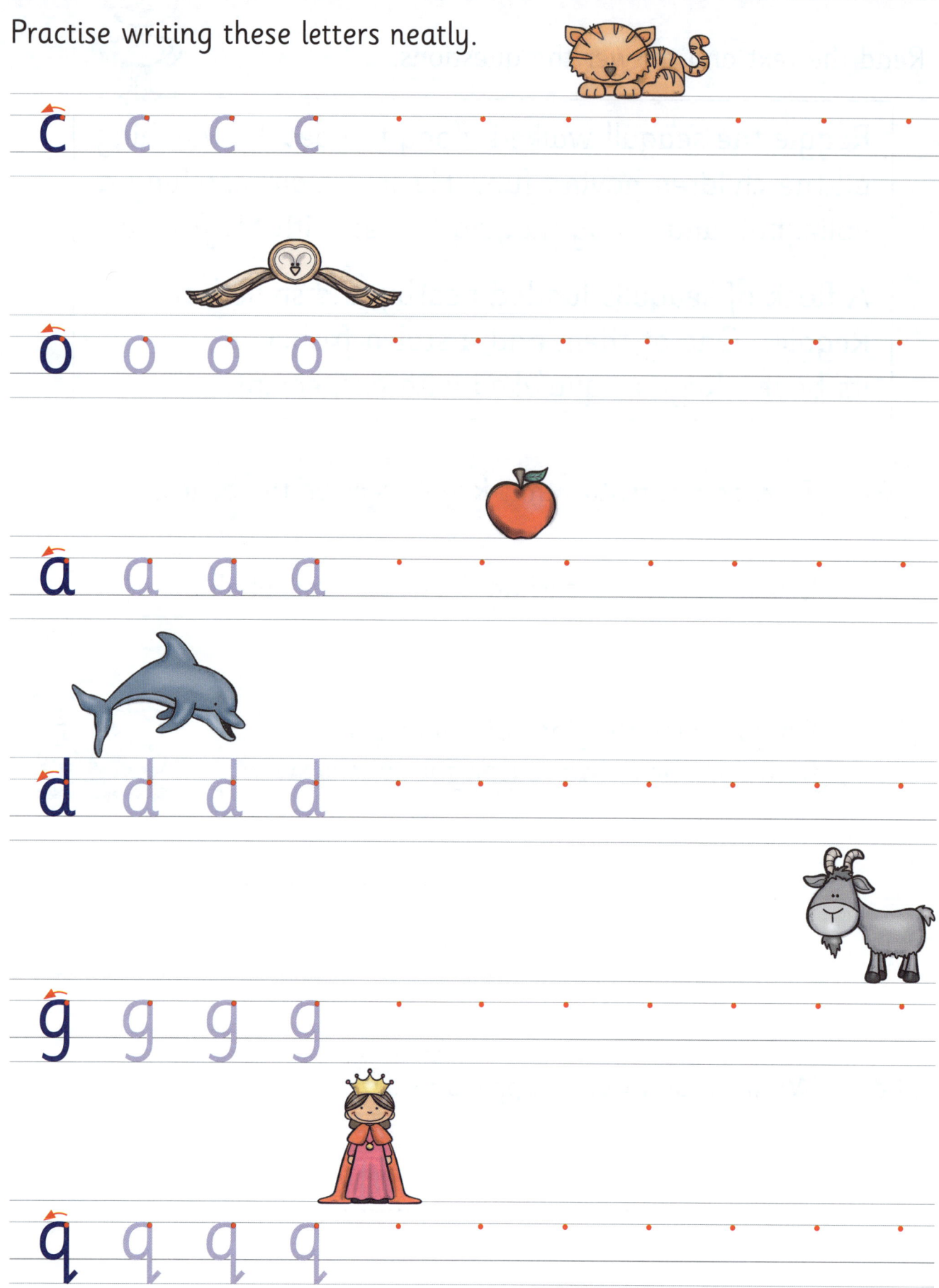

Writing Lower-Case Letters

Practise writing these letters neatly.

h h h h

b b b b

k k k k

r r r r

n n n n

m m m m

p p p p

Section Five — Writing

Writing Lower-Case Letters

Practise writing these letters neatly.

Section Five — Writing

Writing Lower-Case Letters

Practise writing these letters neatly.

e e e e

s s s s

f f f f

v v v v

w w w w

x x x x

z z z z

Section Five — Writing

Writing Capital Letters and Numbers

Practise writing these capital letters neatly.

Section Five — Writing

Writing Capital Letters and Numbers

Practise writing these capital letters and numbers neatly.

S S   T T   U U

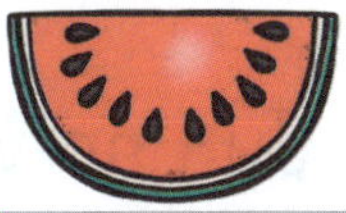

V V   W W

X X   Y Y   Z Z

0 0   1 1

2 2   3 3

4 4   5 5

6 6   7 7

8 8   9 9

Section Five — Writing

Writing Stories

1 Here is the **beginning**, **middle** and **end** of a story. **Draw lines** to match each sentence to its correct place in the story.

Jun nervously waited for the race to start.

Jun crossed the finish line and won the race.

The whistle went off and Jun ran as fast as he could.

beginning

middle

end

2 **Read** this sentence, then **rewrite** it so that it makes sense.

She grinned her at mice.

....

3 Create a story character who is a **pirate**. **Write down** their **name** and give them some **likes** and **dislikes**.

Name: ....

Likes: ....

Dislikes: ....

Section Five — Writing

Writing Stories

4 **Write** the next sentence of each story.

You can write anything you like, as long as it follows on from the first sentence.

Moe woke up to see a monster staring at him.

....

....

The astronaut landed on Mars and looked around.

....

....

Arthur swam deeper and deeper into the ocean.

....

....

Now try this

Read each of your sentences from Question 4 out loud. Do they make sense? If not, rewrite them on a separate piece of paper and try to correct your mistakes.

Describing Things

1 **Colour** the words which describe each picture.

| funny | dark |
| scary | colourful |

| green | busy |
| rainy | sunny |

2 **Read** the sentences. **Fill in** the gaps with a suitable **describing word**. Use a different word each time.

You can choose any word you like, as long as it fits in the sentence.

The .... girl smiled at me.

Sid enjoyed the .... meal.

Priti laughed at the .... clown.

The .... boy began to cry.

Section Five — Writing

Describing Things

3 **Write three** words in the boxes to describe each animal. The first word has been written for you.

The tiger is:

| fluffy | .... | .... |

The giraffe is:

| .... | .... | .... |

4 **Write** about a **different** animal. Try to describe what it **looks like**.

....

....

....

....

Now try this

Describe your favourite place in the world out loud.
You could talk about what you can see, hear or smell.

Section Five — Writing

Writing About Real Life

Warm Up Question

Tick the option which goes at the **start** of a **letter**.

Dear Alexander, ☐

From Lucia ☐

1 **Read** these sentences and **rewrite** them so they make sense.

How your week was?

....

I am writing to thank you say.

....

2 **Draw** lines to **match** each sentence from an **information text** to the **correct topic**.

Some penguins are from Antarctica.

Milk is good for your bones and teeth.

Most bees live together in hives.

Milk

Bees

Penguins

Section Five — Writing

Writing About Real Life

3 Maria is writing a **letter** to her grandad, to say thank you for taking her to the beach. **Fill in** the gaps to help Maria finish her letter.

Dear Grandad,

Thank you for ....

....

It was ....

....

From Maria

4 **Write** out a set of **instructions** for **washing your hands**. The first one has been done for you.

1. Turn on the tap.

....

....

....

....

....

End of Year One Test

1 **Draw lines** to **match** the words to make **compound words**. Then write each **compound word** on the line.

foot   ball   ....

bed   yard   ....

farm   room   ....

3 marks

2 **Circle** the correct spelling of the word in **bold** to complete each sentence.

We **sor / saw** a rainbow this morning.

Charlie began to **whisper / wisper** .

Please **save / saiv** me a seat in the theatre.

3 marks

3 **Cross out** the **two** words that are spelt **incorrectly**.

family   scin   sketch

high   asck

2 marks

End of Year One Test

4 **Join** this pair of sentences using '**and**'.
Write out the new sentence on the lines.

He cooks the meal. I wash the dishes.

....

....

1 mark

5 **Tick** the **two** sentences that use **capital letters** and **full stops** correctly.

Freddy and i are best friends ☐

Zola likes to play table tennis. ☐

we went to. the museum today. ☐

I want to be a dentist one day. ☐

2 marks

6 **Rewrite** this sentence using **capital letters** and either a **question mark** or an **exclamation mark**.

how happy sophie is

....

3 marks

End of Year One Test

Read the story and answer the questions.

> Daisy's goldfish, Jupiter, had always been able to talk. At first it was pretty annoying. Jupiter was very chatty. But Daisy soon got used to it.
>
> Now, Jupiter had picked up a new habit — she was learning to sing. Every night, Jupiter would warble and wail loudly, keeping Daisy wide awake.
>
> One night, Daisy came up with an idea. She decided to sneak into her little brother's room and place Jupiter's tank onto his desk. From then on, Daisy slept peacefully!

7 **Circle** the correct option to complete each sentence.

Daisy was **excited / annoyed** by Jupiter's talking.

Jupiter is learning to **swim / sing** .

She practises her new habit every **week / night** .

3 marks

8 Do you think Daisy likes Jupiter's singing? Give a **reason** for your answer.

....

....

1 mark

End of Year One Test

9 Where does Daisy put Jupiter's tank? **Circle one**.

1 mark

10 What does the word '**sneak**' mean in the text? **Tick one** box.

creep ☐   run ☐   jump ☐

1 mark

11 **Look** at this picture of Daisy. **Write two** words to describe her.

....

....

2 marks

12 **Write** a sentence about how you would **feel** if you met an animal who could talk.

....

....

2 marks

Score: ☐ /24

Answers

Pages 2-5 — Start of Year One Test

1)
   (1 mark for each correct answer)

2)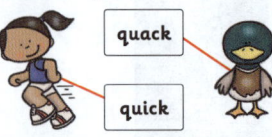
   (1 mark for both correct)

3)
   (1 mark for each correct answer)

4)
   (1 mark for each correct answer)

5) **S**carlett loves toast**.**
   Yusuf is out today**.**
   (1 mark for each correct sentence)

6) plant, splash
   (1 mark for each correct answer)

7) Jack is looking at that map.
   We are at the funfair.
   (1 mark for each correct answer)

8) a — The king has a crown.
   b — She is singing a song today.
   c — That is her little kitten.
   (1 mark for one or two correct,
   2 marks for all correct)

9) 2, 1, 3 (1 mark for each correct answer)

10) Any sensible answers, e.g.
    The cupcake is **pretty** and **yummy**.
    The girl is **happy** and **muddy**.
    (1 mark for each word)

Section One — Grammar

Pages 6-7 — Forming Sentences

Warm Up: I play with my cat.

1) Henry very sleeps well. — No
   Kate makes lots of food. — Yes
2) I wash my hands.
   Dogs can do tricks.
3) Rashid **sails a** boat.
   Lucy **throws the** ball.
4) The plane took off.
   She is very kind.

Page 8 — Joining Words with 'and'

1) Her hair ~~and~~ is short and curly.
   The dragon has ~~and~~ a tail and wings.
   I play ~~and~~ rugby and football.
   Tim loves ~~and~~ hamsters and gerbils.
2) Henry **and** Meera are doctors.
   The sky is grey **and** cloudy.
   Lola plays the trumpet **and** the piano.

Page 9 — Joining Sentences with 'and'

1) She was born in May and he was born in June.
   I fell over at the park and I hurt my knee.
   James went to the zoo and he saw a lion.
2) Samira likes apples **and** Josh likes pears.
   The teacher is speaking **and** they are listening.

Page 10 — Mixed Grammar Practice

1) Mia and Priya are best friends. — Yes
   I wear and a hat gloves. — No
   My dress is green and stripy. — Yes
2) Liam makes a large snowman.
3) I kicked the ball **and** it flew over the fence.

Section Two — Punctuation

Page 11 — Capital Letters for Names and 'I'

1) Freya loves Bert.
   I live in London.
   It is Monday.
   Tom and I are tall.
2) Sanjana went to <u>w</u>ales with Ben.
   Julia had a party on <u>s</u>aturday.
   Peter and <u>i</u> live in Oxford.
3) **S**am and **O**mar read books.

Page 12 — Capital Letters and Full Stops

1) Mum works in a museum. — Yes
   my house is on a big hill. — No
   Jenny. is an amazing person. — No
2) My arm is sore.
   Matt wants a biscuit.
3) **T**he tractor has huge wheels**.**

Page 13 — Separating Words with Spaces

1) My shoes are muddy.
   It is a tasty pie.
2) Jake wins a gold medal.
   I ride my bike to school.
   Milly hides behind a wall.

Answers

Pages 14-15 — Question Marks and Exclamation Marks

Warm Up: The question mark (left) should be red and the exclamation mark (right) should be blue.

1) Where are you**?**
   The clown is funny**.**
   Wes is one year old**.**
   Who is that man**?**
   Lea's hat is blue**.**
   How is the weather**?**

2) I am so happy
   It is such a nice day
   What a strange hat
   How fun this is

3) What a good climber Rob is**!**
   How high is that wall**?**
   How very brave Rob is**!**
   When can I try rock climbing**?**

4) Do you like my wellies**?**
   How far away are you**?**
   What a large chicken this is**!**

Pages 16-17 — Mixed Punctuation Practice

1) Shewalks for miles. — No
   Rahman boils the kettle. — Yes
   Whata good idea! — No
   I had a great day. — Yes

2) Paris, Aisha, Scotland, Luke, February

3) Her brother <u>frank</u> is the chef**.**
   They are always busy on <u>friday</u> evenings**.**
   Mum and <u>i</u> love the pizzas at the restaurant**.**

4) **W**hen does the train leave**?**
   How bright that star is**!**
   Why is **A**lexis so cross**?**

Section Three — Spelling

Page 18 — The Alphabet

Warm Up: k

1) d — consonant, u — vowel, g — consonant
2) tr**i**p, h**u**g, l**a**mp

Page 19 — Consonant Pairs

1) **dr**ess, **sl**ug, **pl**um
2) **cr**ab, **pl**ane, **cr**ime, **gl**ue, **tr**ain, **sk**ip

Pages 20-23 — Vowel Sounds

1) cr**a**ne, m**ai**l, pl**ay**
2) I must b**oi**l the kettle.
   She enj**oy**s running.
   My brother is ann**oy**ing.
   Drums are n**oi**sy.
3) sh**ie**ld, lad**y**, bab**y**, dr**ea**m, th**ie**f

4) My rucksack is quite **light**.
   Taj **tried** to climb the fence.
5) You should have crossed out: flewe, gloo, chue
6) We are travelling on a b**oat**.
   The dog can't find his b**one**.
7) You should have crossed out: wul, mune, rools
8) h**ea**d, p**e**ncil, fr**ow**n, l**ou**d
9) I saw a flow**er** in the garden.
   My sister has c**ur**ly hair.
   Timmy is covered in d**ir**t.
10) alarm, draw, sore, launch
11) Can you **heer** the music? — No
    We are working in **pares**. — No
    The **bear** has brown fur. — Yes
    The shop is **near** the cinema. — Yes

Page 24 — The 'ch', 'sh' and 'th' Sounds

Warm Up: sh

1) fi**sh**, lun**ch**, **th**umb
2) **ch**eese, **sh**eep, ba**th**

Page 25 — Words with 'ph' and 'wh'

1) dol**ph**in, **w**eekend
2) I can say the **alphabet** backwards.
   The **water** is very cold today.
   Use the **whisk** to mix the eggs.
3) **wh**ale, **ph**one, **ph**oto, **wh**eelchair

Page 26 — The Hard 'c' Sound

1) You should have crossed out: sik, korn, sok
2) s**c**ale, tra**ck**
3) carrot, kitten, actor, lucky

Page 27 — Words Ending in 'ff', 'll', 'ss' and 'zz'

1) leaf, hill, sniff
2) fi**zz**, che**ss**, gra**ss**

Page 28 — Words Ending in 've' and 'nk'

1) tank, drink, behave
2) The witch lived in a dark **cave**.
   Harmony cleaned the **sink**.
   I bit a **chunk** out of the apple.
   Larry has **twelve** pairs of sunglasses.
3) drive, shove

Page 29 — Words Ending in 'tch' and 'ch'

1) He uses a cru**tch** to help him walk.
   Karina couldn't rea**ch** the top shelf.
   Galia waited for the chicks to ha**tch**.
2) The monkey swings on the bran**ch**.
   I play fe**tch** with my dog at the park.
   Julia is relaxing on the bea**ch**.

Answers

Page 30 — Adding 's' and 'es' to Words
1) You should have crossed out: peachs, coates
2) path**s**, splash**es**, dragon**s**, tent**s**, fox**es**, cross**es**
3) boxes, apples, dresses

Page 31 — Adding 'ing', 'ed', 'er' and 'est' to Words
1) Tina is **braver** than Victor.
   The birds are **singing** in the trees.
   Hattie has the **neatest** handwriting.
   We **waited** outside the cinema.
2) smallest, cooking, wanted, quicker

Page 32 — Adding 'un' to the Start of Words
1) untie
2) **un**fit, **un**tidy, **un**fold
3) The creaky ladder looked very **unsafe**.
   The **unhappy** pig walked home slowly.
   "That is so **unfair**!" shouted Frances.

Page 33 — Syllables and Compound Words
1) cabin — 2, lake — 1, sand — 1
2) coconut — 3, wood — 1, walrus — 2,
   banana — 3, unicorn — 3, doctor — 2
3) lunchbox, skateboard, blackberry

Pages 34-35 — Tricky Words
Warm Up: your
1) once, love
2) Malaya asked **what** I wanted to eat.
   The **little** mouse hid from the cat.
3) My best <u>frend</u> lives on a farm.
4) move, house, pretty
5) Jakub walks to **school** in the morning.
   I could not remember **where** it was.
   The teacher **said** it was lunchtime.

Pages 36-38 — Mixed Spelling Practice
1) higher, kindest, faster
2) The shop sells cakes, pies and br**ea**d.
   I enjoyed the stor**y** about robots.
   Anwar was very m**ea**n to his brother.
3) in**ch**, mar**ch**, pa**tch**, swi**tch**
4) str**aw**, h**ow**l, d**ai**sy, cowb**oy**
5) umbrella**s**, witch**es**, bus**es**
6) You should have crossed out:
   microfone, whedding, phantastic
7) wear, stole, right
8) n**urse**, s**tick**

Pages 39-41 — Progress Test 1
1) My brother is intelligent and kind.
   The bee has black and yellow stripes.
   (1 mark for each correct answer)
2) **ch**ild, **th**rone, fre**sh**
   (1 mark for one correct,
   2 marks for two or three correct)
3) treat, scene, care, bite
   (1 mark for each correct answer)
4) You should have crossed out:
   walkked, jumpped, stayying
   (1 mark for each word crossed out)
5) shell, cute, five (1 mark for each correct answer)
6) dishes, plants, catch
   (1 mark for each correct answer)
7) The weather is terrible **today**.
   Li **unwraps** his presents.
   Would you like **some** vegetables?
   (1 mark for each correct answer)
8) What a funny film that was! — Yes
   What size are your new boots! — No
   What do you want for lunch? — Yes
   (1 mark for each correct answer)
9) **A**my had a party on **F**riday**.**
   (1 mark for each correct answer)

Section Four — Reading

Pages 42-43 — Finding Information
Raj's Day Out
1) the beach
2) Raj — sandcastle
   Grace — ice cream
   Cole — book
3) Any sensible answer, e.g. They paddled in the sea.

Facts about Kangaroos
1) Kangaroos live in **Australia**.
   A **mob** is a group of kangaroos.
2) They have strong legs.
3) Any sensible answer, e.g. In their pouches.

Pages 44-45 — Thinking About Words
The Treehouse
1) looked
2) quickly
3) frightened

Dear Diary
1) big
2) happily
3) noisily
4) wonderful

Answers

Pages 46-47 — Making Assumptions
Warm Up: Sophie **likes** animals.
1) The weather is cold outside.
   Meena thought Benjamin's joke was funny.
   Elizabeth likes spiders.
2) Chloe is going to a dance lesson.
   Hassan has just finished a race.
   Esther enjoys the autumn.
3) red

Pages 48-49 — Putting Things in Order
1) serve — 3, decorate — 2
   peel — 2, eat — 3, grow — 1
2) sheep — 2, pigs — 1, horse — 3
3) pasta — 2, soup — 1, cherries — 4, salad — 3
4) They found treasure buried in the sand. — 3
   They arrived and began to explore. — 2
   The pirates set sail for the island. — 1
5) Thomas ate a big sandwich for his lunch. — 3
   Thomas walked to the park to meet his friends. — 1
   Thomas played with his basketball. — 2
   Any sensible answer, e.g. Thomas danced.

Pages 50-51 — What Happens Next?
1) He eats a cookie.
2) She washes the car.
3) Any sensible answer, e.g. The chick hatches.
4) Any sensible answer, e.g. She crosses the river in the boat.
5) Any sensible answer, e.g. He goes home.

Pages 52-54 — Mixed Practice — Stories
Ava and the Robot
1) two years
2) Any sensible answer, e.g. Because it is the first robot she has ever built.
3) Any sensible answer, e.g. To cook her favourite meal.

Little Red Riding Hood
1) Any sensible answer, e.g. To visit her grandmother.
2) fruit, bread
3) walking

The Alien
1) tired
2) puts on her pyjamas, brushes her teeth
3) tiny

Pages 55-57 — Mixed Practice — Information Texts
How to Grow a Plant
1) You should have circled the flowerpot and the seeds
2) water, sunshine
3) Any sensible answer, e.g. A green shoot coming out of the soil.

Octopuses
1) Octopuses live in **all** oceans.
   Octopuses have eight **long** arms.
2) Any two of clams, crabs and small fish.
3) Any sensible answer, e.g. To hide from other sea creatures.

Who were the Vikings?
1) The Vikings were from **Scandinavia**.
   Viking longships were made from **wood**.
2) The Vikings were good at sailing.
3) Any sensible answer, e.g. Because they spent so much time at sea.

Pages 58-59 — Mixed Practice — Poems
The Little Brown Mouse
1) brown, little
2) searching
3) Any sensible answer, e.g. The mouse eats the beans, because it thinks they are a treat.

Spring
1) chilly
2) bird — 3
   sun — 1
   flower — 2
3) Any sensible answer, e.g. Yes, because the narrator calls it "wonderful".

Pages 60-63 — Progress Test 2
1) Would you like a pi**zz**a?
   He accepted her kind o**ff**er.
   The bee is bu**zz**ing loudly.
   (1 mark for each correct answer)
2) I climb up the tree. (1 mark)
3) My aunt got me a **doll** as a present.
   He **kicked** the ball as hard as he could.
   The dress was red with **white** stripes.
   (1 mark for each correct answer)
4) He is the fast**est** runner I know.
   I am much tall**er** than I was last year.
   Fatima is the old**est** in her class.
   (1 mark for each correct answer)
5) think, trunk (1 mark for each correct answer)

Answers

6) You want to visit the zoo. (1 mark)
7) The tree is in **the woods**.
   The writer wants to be **taller**.
   (1 mark for each correct answer)
8) giggle (1 mark)
9) very big (1 mark)
10) frisbee, volleyball (1 mark for each correct answer)
11) Any sensible answer, e.g.
    Yes, because they smiled at Reggie. (1 mark)
12) Any sensible answer, e.g.
    The seagulls all play frisbee together. (1 mark)

Section Five — Writing

Pages 70-71 — Writing Stories

1) Jun nervously waited for the race
   to start. — beginning
   Jun crossed the finish line and won the race. — end
   The whistle went off and Jun ran as
   fast as he could. — middle
2) She grinned at her mice.
3) Any sensible answers, e.g.
   Name: **Davey McDoom**
   Likes: **His pet parrot**
   Dislikes: **Storms**
4) Any sensible answers, e.g.
   Moe woke up to see a monster staring at him.
   He screamed loudly and ran away.
   The astronaut landed on Mars and looked around.
   She saw lots of shining stars.
   Arthur swam deeper and deeper into the ocean.
   It was cold and dark but he wasn't afraid.

Pages 72-73 — Describing Things

1) dark, scary, green, sunny
2) Any sensible answers, e.g.
   The **happy** girl smiled at me.
   Sid enjoyed the **tasty** meal.
   Priti laughed at the **funny** clown.
   The **sad** boy began to cry.
3) Any sensible answers, e.g.
   The tiger is: angry, orange
   The giraffe is: spotty, happy, cute
4) Any sensible answer, e.g. Elephants are huge
   and grey. They have long trunks and big ears.

Pages 74-75 — Writing About Real Life

Warm Up: Dear Alexander,

1) Any sensible answers, e.g.
   How was your week?
   I am writing to say thank you.

2) Some penguins are from Antarctica. — Penguins
   Milk is good for your bones and teeth. — Milk
   Most bees live together in hives. — Bees
3) Any sensible answer, e.g.
   Dear Grandad,
   Thank you for **taking me to the beach.**
   It was **really fun.**
   From Maria
4) Any sensible answer, e.g.
   1. Turn on the tap.
   2. **Cover your hands in soap.**
   3. **Scrub your hands in the water.**
   4. **Turn off the tap.**
   5. **Dry your hands.**

Pages 76-79 — End of Year One Test

1) football, bedroom, farmyard
   (1 mark for each correct answer)
2) We **saw** a rainbow this morning.
   Charlie began to **whisper**.
   Please **save** me a seat in the theatre.
   (1 mark for each correct answer)
3) You should have crossed out: scin and asck
   (1 mark for each word crossed out)
4) He cooks the meal **and** I wash the dishes. (1 mark)
5) Zola likes to play table tennis.
   I want to be a dentist one day.
   (1 mark for each correct answer)
6) **H**ow happy **S**ophie is**!**
   (1 mark for each correct capital
   letter and exclamation mark)
7) Daisy was **annoyed** by Jupiter's talking.
   Jupiter is learning to **sing**.
   She practises her new habit every **night**.
   (1 mark for each correct answer)
8) Any sensible answer, e.g.
   No, because it keeps Daisy awake. (1 mark)
9)  (1 mark)
10) creep (1 mark)
11) Any sensible answers, e.g. happy and blonde
    (1 mark for each correct answer)
12) Any sensible answer, e.g. I would feel surprised
    but also very excited. (1 mark for a short answer,
    2 marks for a more developed answer)